AF589352

TO WALLACE AND DOROTHY, MY FAVORITE LITTLE TROLLS - JJ

FOR BENSON, WHO TAUGHT ME HOW TO HAVE FUN - MM

First edition 2026

ISBN 979-8-9933131-0-8 (print)
ISBN 979-8-9933131-1-5 (ebook)

Library of Congress Control Number: 2025922087

This book was typeset in Tarzana Nar OT Regular.
The artwork was created with gouache and colored pencil and digitally edited.

THE LEGEND OF THE Bogus Basin Troll

Written by Jordan Jacobs

Illustrated by Meah Matthews

There once was a troll
who lived on Bogus Basin Road.
He's lived there 50 years,
or so we've all been told.

His home is beneath the cattle guard at mile-marker number four.
He hitches a ride to the ski resort when a passenger opens up their door.

BOGUS
GOLD

SLOW

It is said that if you drive him up the mountain
he'll keep you safe the whole day through,
while everyone has fun skiing and snowboarding, too.

The next time you're heading up for some fun on the slopes,
make sure to let the troll hop inside, never giving up his hopes.

My family has always practiced this tradition,
never forgetting to give the troll a ride.

We open our doors at the cattle guard,
"Thanks for picking me up," he grins, quite satisfied.

It's 16 miles up the road, winding around 172 curves.
Everyone looks out the windows,
DOUGLAS FIR!
PONDEROSA!
WESTERN WHITE PINE!
TAMARACK!
admiring the various
species of conifers.

Once at Bogus Basin, we shuffle to get in line to take the Coach chairlift.
Warming up our bodies on the greens is always such a gift.

Now we're ready for a greater challenge. We head towards Deer Point Express.
Riding the lift to the top of the mountain,
"I'm feeling nervous," I confess.

At the top of the lift, skis and boards pointed up, we get off the chair.
Take a deep breath and say to each other,
"Shred the gnar and get some air!"

We're going down Shaker Ridge.
OH NO! I'm skiing towards a tree!
I hear someone shout,
"PIZZA!"
and I quickly turn my skis into the letter V.

My skis stop me just in time.

PHEW! I was protected.

I wonder how I got so lucky.

Maybe it was the troll keeping me safe, I suspected.

Our stomachs start to rumble as we approach the bottom of the hill. We head over to the lodge for a bite to eat from Bogus Creek Grill.

After lunch we hit a few more runs. We have no more energy remaining.

“Ugh! Can you hold my skis? My feet hurt,” my little brother was complaining.

We make our way to the parking lot, gently tossing our gear into the car.
Heading back down the mountain we're glad to know home isn't too far.

The troll expresses gratitude when we see mile-marker number four.
We slow to a gentle roll then open the passenger door.

He tells us, “Great job today
carving through all the fresh powder.”

we scream back a little louder.

Home at last.
I get into bed,
feeling happy deep in my soul.

Goodness, I'm glad to know
the legend of the Bogus Basin troll.

Jordan Jacobs is an educator, mom, and lifelong learner who believes that stories are one of the best ways to experience new perspectives and emotions. A graduate of the University of Texas at Austin, her love for education was nurtured by her family and the influence of wonderful teachers throughout her youth. She lives in Boise, Idaho, with her partner Anthony and their two children. She values preserving traditions which inspired her to write her debut children's book, The Legend of the Bogus Basin Troll.

Each year, 10% of the book's net proceeds go to a local 501(c)(3).

Meah Matthews is an artist from Boise, Idaho influenced by all things colorful, whimsical, and joyous, with a certain penchant for nostalgia. When she's not creating, she can be found loudly playing vinyl records while her three daughters and two dogs play louder, or looking at dinner menus for her next restaurant date with the love of her life.

Meah believes that picture books are for readers of all ages, and that people of all ages can be readers.

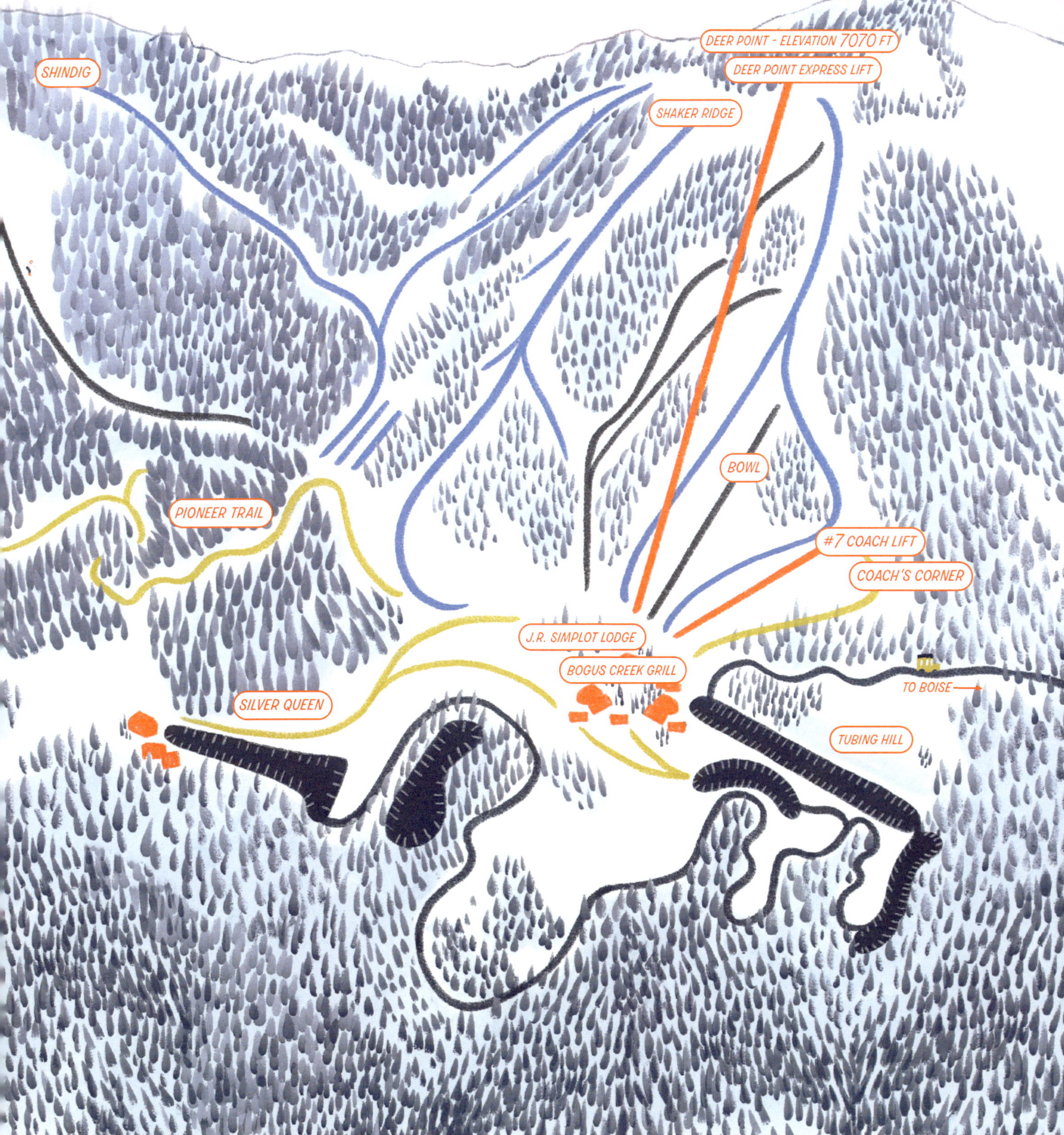

DEER POINT - ELEVATION 7070 FT
DEER POINT EXPRESS LIFT
SHINDIG
SHAKER RIDGE
BOWL
PIONEER TRAIL
#7 COACH LIFT
COACH'S CORNER
J.R. SIMPLOT LODGE
BOGUS CREEK GRILL
SILVER QUEEN
TO BOISE
TUBING HILL

www.ingramcontent.com/pod-product-compliance
Ingram Content Group UK Ltd.
Pitfield, Milton Keynes, MK11 3LW, UK
UKRC032027290726
14090UKWH00008B/488